FIDELITY

THICH NHAT HANH

PARALLAX PRESS

FIDELITY

*How to Create a Loving
Relationship That Lasts*

Parallax Press
P.O. Box 7355
Berkeley, California 94707

Parallax Press is the publishing division
of Unified Buddhist Church

This book uses material from talks given in Vietnamese and English
by Zen Master Thich Nhat Hanh in 2010 and 2011.

Edited by Rachel Neumann
Cover and text design by Jess Morphew

Library of Congress Cataloging-in-Publication Data

Nhât Hanh, Thích.
  Fidelity : how to strengthen and nourish our intimate relationships / Thích Nhât Hanh.
     p. cm.
  ISBN 978-1-935209-91-1
  1. Love--Religious aspects--Buddhism. 2. Sex--Religious aspects--Buddhism. 3.
Buddhism--Doctrines. 4. Tipitaka. Suttapitaka. Khuddakanikaya. Dhammapada--Criticism,
interpretation, etc. I. Title.
  BQ4570.L6N52 2011
  205'.63--dc23
                                    2011019198

1 2 3 4 5 / 15 14 13 12 11

As light as a cloud or fine water grass
Yet it can fill or empty the ocean of love

—NGUYEN DU, *Tale of Kieu*

CONTENTS

CHAPTER I

TRUE LOVE

IN THE SITTING ROOM OF THE WESTERN Heaven Temple in Hue, Vietnam, there are a pair of wooden panels that the monks have inscribed with two lines of verse.

Without worldly manners, with the bones of an immortal
The heart of the Buddha has great love.

This verse means that the Buddha is a loving person. The kind of love that the Buddha teaches is a love that is very wide and inclusive. Thanks to his great love, the Buddha could embrace the whole world.

When Siddhartha became a Buddha, he didn't cease to be a person who needed to give and receive love. In the Buddha, just as in all of us, there were the seeds of sensual desire. He left home at the age of twenty-nine and attained enlightenment at the age of thirty-five. Thirty-five is still very young. Most of us still have a lot of sensual desire at that age. The Buddha had enough love, as well as enough mental responsibility and awakening, to be able to manage his sexual energy. We can do this as well.

This doesn't mean that we don't feel sensual desire; we do. But we aren't overtaken by that feeling. Instead, we can act from a broader feeling of love.

Love has its roots to some extent in sensual desire. Sensual desire has the capacity to become love in all of us. Mindfulness practice doesn't sweep away or bring an end to sensual desire. To bring such a thing to an end would make us no longer human. We practice in order to have the capacity to deal with desire, to smile with desire, so that we may be free from it.

All human beings have the seeds of sensual desire within. Now and then, when it returns, we can use our mindfulness and insight to smile at that desire. Then, we won't be overwhelmed by sensual desire, and we won't get trapped.

Love can bring us happiness and peace as long as we love in such a way that we don't make a net to confine ourselves and others. We can tell the correct way to love because, when we love correctly, we don't create more suffering.

The Buddha spoke about this in a teaching called "The Net of Sensual Love."* The word "love" in this sutra has a somewhat negative connotation. To be caught by sensual love is to be like a fish that swims into a trap and can't escape. In the sutra, the image of a net is used to describe the loss of freedom when someone is caught and entangled by sensual desire.

---

*See the Appendix for the complete text of the sutra.

The Sutra on the Net of Sensual Love uses two characters to signify love. The first means not only the romantic love between two people, but also a love for humanity. This character doesn't mean attachment; it means true love. The second character means craving, covetousness, or desire. When the two characters occur separately it's very easy to translate them: on the one side there is love and on the other side there is desire. When we put the words together, it describes a love that contains desire.

Although the Buddha initially taught the Sutra on the Net of Sensual Love to monastics, it is relevant for everyone. People often ask if it is difficult to be a celibate monk or nun, but to practice mindfulness as a monastic is in many ways easier than to practice as a layperson. To refrain from sexual activity altogether is much easier than to have a healthy sexual relationship. As monastics, we spend our time in practice and in nature. We don't watch television, read romantic novels, or look at images in movies or magazines that give rise to sensual desire. Meanwhile, laypeople are always bombarded with images and music that feed sexual craving. To have all that stimulus and still have a healthy sexual relationship with mutual understanding and love, you need constant practice.

We are all motivated by love. Love can be our greatest joy or—when it gets confused with craving and attachment—our greatest suffering. By understanding the roots of our suffering and learning how to develop deep understanding of ourselves and our loved one, we can enjoy the relaxation, joy, and peace that come from true love.

CHAPTER 2

INTIMACY

> Just as a monkey jumps from one tree to another, so people jump from one prison of sensual love to another.
>
> —Sutra on the Net of Sensual Love, Verse 9

WE MIGHT RECOGNIZE OURSELVES in this image of the monkey. If we don't like something our partner does, we just find another partner. Then, when that partner inevitably does something we don't like, we move on to the next.

We all want love and understanding, but we often confuse love with desire. Love and desire are different. When they get mixed up together, we need to look at them deeply and make an effort to sort them out! There are three kinds of intimacy: physical, emotional, and spiritual. Physical intimacy can't be separated from emotional intimacy; we always feel some emotional intimacy when we're sexual, even if we profess not to. When spiritual intimacy is there, then physical and emotional intimacy can be healthy, healing, and pleasurable.

EMOTIONAL INTIMACY

Every one of us is seeking emotional intimacy. We want to be in harmony. We want to have real communication and mutual understanding. Although physical desire is not love, it is impossible to have physical intimacy without emotional intimacy because body and mind are not two separate entities. What happens in the body will have an effect on the mind and vice versa. The mind can't exist without a body to hold it and the body relies on the mind to move and to function. There should be no distinction between respecting your body and respecting your mind, because your body is you. Your loved one's body is also her mind. You can't respect one part of her without respecting the other.

I know a musician who for many years went out to parties every weekend to listen to music, drink, and dance. At the beginning of the evening, these parties would be joyful and open-hearted. People would be smiling and relating to one another. But near midnight, people would close up. They started focusing only on finding someone to bring home with them that night. The music, alcohol, and the food watered seeds of sexual desire in them. The next morning, many of them would wake up next to a virtual stranger. They would say good-bye and part ways, without remembering what they had shared in body and mind in private the night before. The following week, he would go through the same cycle again at another party. But no matter how many parties he went to or how many people he slept with, he couldn't find the emotional well-being he was seeking, or fill the void he felt inside.

PHYSICAL INTIMACY

Every living thing wants to continue into the future. This is true of humans, as well as of all other animals. Sex and sexual reproduction are part of life. Sex can bring great pleasure and enrich a deep connection between two people. We shouldn't be against sex, but we also shouldn't confuse it with love. True love doesn't necessarily have to do with sex. We can love perfectly without sex and we can have sex without love.

Spiritual awakening isn't the exclusive provenance of celibacy. There are people who are celibate but who don't have enough mindfulness, concentration, and insight. When people in intimate relationships have mindfulness, concentration, and insight, their relationships have an element of holiness. Sexual intimacy shouldn't occur before there is communion, understanding, and sharing on the emotional and spiritual level.

The human body is beautiful. The tree, the flower, the snow, the river, and the willow are also beautiful. We are surrounded by beauty, including the humans and animals that populate the Earth. But we have to learn how to treat beauty so that we don't destroy it.

Our society is organized in such a way that sensual pleasure seems the most important thing. Producers and manufacturers want to sell their products. So they advertise their goods and water the seed of craving in you. They want you to be caught by the desire for sensual pleasure.

When we're lonely and cut off, when we suffer and need healing, that is the time to come home to ourselves. We may also need to be close to another person. But if, right away, we're sexually intimate with someone we've just met, that relationship won't heal or warm us. It will just be a distraction. When we're trapped by sensual love, we spend our time worrying that the other person will leave or betray us.

Loneliness can't be dissipated by sexual activity. You can't heal yourself by having sex. You have to learn how to be comfortable with yourself and focus on making your own home within. Once you have a spiritual path, you have a home. Once you can deal with your emotions and handle the difficulties of your daily life, then you have something to offer to another person. The other person has to do the same thing. Both people have to heal on their own so they feel at ease in themselves; then they can become a home for each other. Otherwise, all that we share in physical intimacy is our loneliness and suffering.

SPIRITUAL INTIMACY

Spirituality doesn't mean a belief in a specific spiritual teaching. Everyone needs a spiritual dimension in his or her life. Without a spiritual dimension, we can't deal with the daily difficulties we encounter. Mindfulness can be an important aspect of your spiritual path, whether or not you are a religious practitioner.

Your spiritual practice can help you deal with your strong emotions. It can help you to listen to and embrace your own suffering, and help you to recognize and embrace the suffering of your partner and loved ones. Spiritual intimacy with your partner helps create emotional intimacy and makes your physical intimacy more fulfilling. The three kinds of intimacy are interconnected.

CHAPTER 3

THE ROOTS
OF DESIRE

> Blinded by attachment, sooner or later we fall into sensual love. Anxiety mounts day by day, just as water fills a pond drop by drop.
>
> —Sutra on the Net of Sensual Love, Verse 3

IF WE CONTINUE TO CULTIVATE sensual love, then inevitably we arrive at sexual craving and desire. We shouldn't underestimate sensual love. When it arises, we should pay attention to it right at the beginning.

Every human being wants to love and be loved. This is very natural. But often love, desire, need, and fear get wrapped up all together. There are so many songs with the words, "I love you; I need you." Such lyrics imply that loving and craving are the same thing, and that the other person is just there to fulfill our needs. We might feel we can't survive without the other person. When we say, "Darling, I can't live without you. I need you," we think we're speaking the language of love. We even feel it's a compliment to the other person. But that need is actually a continuation of the original fear and desire that have been with us since we were small children.

As babies, we were helpless. We had arms and feet, but we couldn't use them to go anywhere. There was very little we could do for ourselves. We went from having been in a very warm, wet, comfortable place inside the womb to being in a cold hard place full of harsh light. In order to breathe our first breath, we had to first expel the liquid from our lungs. It was a dangerous moment.

Our original desire is to survive. And our original fear is that no one will be there to take care of us. Before we could talk or understand language, we knew that the sound of footsteps coming closer meant someone would feed and care for us. This made us happy; we really needed that person.

As newborns, we could distinguish the smell of our mother or the person taking care of us. We knew the sound of her voice. We came to love that smell and that sound. That's the first, original love, born from our need; it's completely natural.

When we grow up and look for a partner, the original desire to survive is still there in many of us. We think that without someone else, we can't survive. We might be looking for a partner, but the child in us is looking for that feeling of safety and comfort we had when our parent or caregiver arrived.

When we were infants, the smell of our mother was the most wonderful smell in the world, because we needed her. In Asia, people use the nose more than the mouth when they kiss each other. They recognize and enjoy the smell of the other person.

We might relax into a relationship, thinking, "I'm okay now, because I have someone to love me and support me." But the infant in us is saying, "Now I can relax; my caregiver is here." That feeling of joy does not come simply from a true appreciation of the presence of the other person. Rather, we are happy and peaceful because with this person we can feel safe and at ease. Later on, when our relationship becomes difficult, we aren't relaxed anymore, and happiness is no longer there.

Fear and desire are connected. Out of our original fear came a desire for the person who made us feel comfortable and safe. An infant feels, "I'm helpless; I have no means to take care of myself. I'm vulnerable. I need someone, otherwise I'll die." Unless we recognize, take care of, and release those feelings, they'll continue to determine the decisions we make. If, as adults, we continue to feel insecure and unsafe, this is the continuation of the original fear that we haven't yet recognized and understood.

NON-FEAR

> When desire stops, there is no more fear. We are then truly free, peaceful, and happy. When the practitioner has no more desire, nor any internal formations, he has freed himself from the abyss.
>
> —Sutra on the Net of Sensual Love, Verse 30

Most of us walk around afraid of separation from our loved ones, afraid of loneliness, and afraid of nothingness. Our greatest fear is that when we die we will become nothing. Many of us believe that our entire existence is only a single life span from the moment we are born until the moment we die. We believe that we are born from nothing and when we die we become nothing.

We get filled with the fear of annihilation. But annihilation is just a notion. Buddha taught that there is no birth; there is no death; there is no coming; there is no going; there is no same; there is no different; there is no permanent self. If we practice meditation, we can generate the energies of mindfulness and concentration. These energies will lead us to the insight that there is no birth and no death. We can truly remove our fear of death. When we understand that we cannot be destroyed, we are liberated from fear. It is a great relief. Non-fear is the ultimate joy.

If you have fear, you can't have happiness. If you're still running after the object of your desire, then you still have fear. The fear goes together with craving. If you stop the craving, the fear will go away naturally.

Sometimes you're fearful, but you don't know why. The Buddha says the reason you're fearful is because you're still craving. If you stop running after the object of your craving, you'll have no fear. Having no fear, you can be peaceful. With peace in your body and mind, you aren't beset by worries and you have fewer accidents. You are free.

One of the greatest gifts we can offer to other people is to embody non-fear and nonattachment. This true teaching is more precious than money or material resources. Fear distorts our lives and makes us miserable. We cling to objects and people, like a drowning person clinging to a floating log. By practicing nonattachment and sharing this wisdom with others, we give the gift of non-fear. Everything is impermanent. This moment passes. That person walks away. Happiness is still possible.

When we love someone, we should look deeply into the nature of that love. True love doesn't contain suffering or attachment. It brings well-being to ourselves and others. True love is generated from within. With true love, you feel complete in yourself; you don't need something from outside. True love is like the sun, shining with its own light, and offering that light to everyone.

CRAVING

The roots of sensual love are deep and firm. The tree may be cut, yet the branches and leaves sprout again.
—Sutra on the Net of Sensual Love, Verse 8

My dear sensual desire, I know your source. The desiring mind comes from wants and wrong perceptions.
—Sutra on the Net of Sensual Love, Verse 31

In verse 31 of the sutra, the Buddha calls our desire by its true name: craving. Although we want love and healing, we still follow our sensual cravings. Why? The craving makes knots in the deeper part of our mind. The internal knots push us. Sometimes we don't want to move, speak, or act like that. But something deep inside us pushes us to speak and act in that way. Afterward, we feel so ashamed. That internal knot is ordering us around. It pushes us to do and say things against our will. And when we've done it, it's too late, and we feel deeply sorry. We say to ourselves, "How could I have said or done that?" But it's already done. The root of that craving is our habit energy. When we look deeply at it, we can begin to untie the knot.

HABIT ENERGY

The mind of sensual love is like a stream of water following the course of habit energy and pride. Our thoughts and perceptions become tainted by the hues of sensual love; we hide the truth from ourselves and cannot see it.

—Sutra on the Net of Sensual Love, Verse 10

Habit energy is there in all of us in the form of seeds transmitted from our ancestors, our grandparents, and our parents, as well as seeds created by the difficulties we ourselves have experienced. Often we're unaware of these energies operating in us. We may want to be in a committed relationship but our habit energies can color our perceptions, direct our behaviors, and make our lives difficult.

With mindfulness, we can become aware of the habit energy that has been passed down to us. We might see that our parents or grandparents were also very weak in similar ways. We can be aware without judgment that our negative habits come from these ancestral roots. We can smile at our shortcomings, at our habit energy.

Perhaps in the past when we've noticed ourselves doing something unintentional, something we may have inherited, we've blamed our individual, isolated selves. With awareness, we can begin to see our actions have deeper roots and we can transform these habit energies.

With the practice of mindfulness, we recognize the habitual nature of our desire. Mindfulness and concentration can help us look and find the roots of our actions. Our actions may have been inspired by something that happened yesterday, or they may have been inspired by something three hundred years old that has its roots in one of our ancestors.

When we're able to smile at a provocation or direct our sexual energy towards something positive, we can be aware of our ability, appreciate it, and continue in this way. The key is to be aware of our actions. Our mindfulness will help us understand where our actions are coming from.

If we aren't yet able to transform that habit energy, we will come out of the prison of one relationship only to fall into the prison of another. It's common practice, when we encounter difficulty and suffering with our partner or spouse, to think we need to separate or divorce. By getting away from the other person, we think we'll have freedom. We think that person is the cause of our suffering. But the truth is that even though we may feel freer right after the divorce or separation, we often get entangled immediately with someone else. We may stick to this new person, but we end up acting just like we did with the last one. We are the victims of our own habits. The way we think, speak, and act has not changed. What we did to cause suffering to the first person, we now do to cause suffering to someone new, and we create a second hell.

But if we are aware of our actions, we can decide whether or not they are beneficial and if not, we can decide not to repeat them. If we're aware of the habit energies in us and can become more intentional in our thoughts, speech, and actions, then we can transform not only ourselves, but also our ancestors who planted the seeds. If we're able to do that, it means our ancestors are also able to smile at what is provoking them. If one person keeps calm and smiles at a provocation, the whole world will have a better chance for peace.

COMPLEXES

Pride is a current that runs along with habit energy. Our pride is often connected to our sense of sexual self-worth. When a person is attracted to us, we have the impression that our self-pride is satisfied. We feel we have some value, some attractiveness, some good qualities and that is why the other person is attached to us. We want to be with someone to prove that we are talented and beautiful. If we're alone, we often think that it's proof that we're not interesting or pretty enough, and we suffer.

We're always comparing. Our thoughts are reinforced by the images we constantly see around us and by our superficial view of others. We think we're better or worse than someone, or else we're focused on trying to be equal to that person. These three complexes—better than, worse than, and equal to—are intimately connected with our sexual energy.

Maintaining our idea of a separate self is the source of all of our complexes. We see ourselves as separate individuals, so we compare ourselves with others to see if we are better, worse, or equal to them. But looking deeply, we see that there is no self with which to compare. Our dualistic thinking is the basis of our attachment and craving.

We have two hands and we have names for them, right hand and left hand. Have you ever seen the two hands fighting each other? I have never seen this. Every time my left hand gets hurt, I notice that my right hand comes naturally to help. So there must be something like love in the body. Sometimes my hands help each other, sometimes they each act separately, but they have never fought.

My right hand invites the bell, writes books, does calligraphy, and pours tea. But my right hand doesn't look down on the left hand and say, "Oh left hand, you are good for nothing. All the poems, I wrote them. All that calligraphy in German, French, and English—I've done it all. You are useless. You are good for nothing." The right hand has never suffered from the complex of pride. The left hand has never suffered from the complex of unworthiness.

It's wonderful. When the right hand has a problem, the left hand comes right away. The right hand never says, "You have to pay me back. I always come to help you. You owe me."

The sutra talks about how the stream of desire flows along with the stream of our complexes. We want to prove that we are someone, that we are worthy, that we have value, so we look for someone to approve of us and in this way we pull others into the suffering caused by attachment. This is a pity. When we can see our partner as not separate from us, not better or worse or even equal to ourselves, then we have the wisdom of nondiscrimination. We see the happiness of others as our happiness, their suffering as our suffering.

Look at your hand. The fingers are like five brothers and sisters of the same family. Suppose we're a family of five. When we remember that if one person suffers, we all suffer, we have the wisdom of nondiscrimination. If the other person is happy, we are also happy.

Very few people know how to see love and romance in terms of impermanence and nonself. Realizing nonself, we can see ourselves in our beloveds, and see them in ourselves. At that point we become healthy, light, and happy. To belittle or praise our loved ones is also to belittle or praise ourselves. Nonself is an insight that can help resolve the problem of sexual desire. Instead of denying love, we can view love in light of the insight of nonself.

To love, in the true sense of the word, is to feel no discrimination. We should have the element of equanimity, so that we can love without boundaries. Equanimity is the absence of the three complexes— better, worse, and equal. We no longer discriminate. We are able to embrace everything and we no longer suffer. When there is love without discrimination, there is also an absence of suffering.

RELEASING CRAVING

The stream of the mind continues to flow freely, allowing the knots of sensual love to burgeon and snag. Only real insight is capable of discerning this reality clearly, helping us to cut through its roots in our mind.

—Sutra on the Net of Sensual Love, Verse 11

Some time after the Buddha was enlightened, he went back to his native kingdom. He saw that the political situation was very bad. His father had already passed away and many of the high government officials were corrupt. Mara, the embodiment of craving, appeared and said, "Buddha, you are the best politician in the world. If you decide to become king, you can save the situation in your native country; you can save the whole world." The Buddha said, "Mara, my old friend, many conditions are needed for the situation to change; it's not just a matter of who is king. I abandoned this kingdom seven years ago in order to practice. Since that time, I have discovered so many things; I can help countless people, many more than I could help if I were to become king."

That pushing desire in each of us is Mara. The Mara inside us says, "You're good; you're the best." But when Mara says these things, we have to recognize that they come from Mara. "I know you; you are my Mara." Each of us has many Maras inside. They come and talk to us. As soon as we recognize that negative energy, we can say, "My dear Mara, I know that you are there. You can't pull me."

When sensual desire arises, you can say, "My dear sensual love, I know your root. You come from desire based on my wrong perceptions. But now I don't have that craving, and you can't touch me. Even if you are there, you can't pull me. I don't have any more wishes, and I have no more wrong perceptions about you. So how can you arise?"

Now you are like the fish who already knows the hook is in the bait. You know the bait isn't a source of nourishment, and you are no longer caught by it. Your perception is clear. You are awakened, and you can't be pulled by this and that.

When we let go of our complexes and look deeply at our habit energy, our cravings disappear. We can undo the ordering energy, the pushing knot. We come out of the abyss. Looking deeply, we understand better. We can undo all the internal knots, and then we are free.

CHAPTER 4

TRANSFORMING LONELINESS AND SUFFERING

EACH OF US HAS A DEEP DESIRE TO know and understand the world and to be known and understood in
return. That is a deep natural thirst. But often this thirst
causes us to wait for something outside of ourselves.

Often, we've had no time to understand ourselves
before we've already found objects for our love. Or, we
continue to wait for something that will make us feel
fulfilled. This is one reason many of us in industrialized
countries are now constantly on our phones or checking
our email.

All of us feel lonely and empty inside sometimes.
When we have these feelings, we try to fill the vacuum
by consuming food or alcohol, or by engaging in sexual
activity. Yet, even while we are enjoying these things,
the empty feeling not only persists but becomes deeper
than before. We can transform this feeling of loneliness only when we truly understand ourselves and our
loved ones.

Even if two people have a baby together, they are
still separate. Each of us remains in isolation. It's not by
living together, or by having sexual relations, or even by
having children together that we can dispel this feeling
of isolation. We can only dispel our mutual isolation
when we practice mindfulness and are able to truly
come home to ourselves and each other.

ATTENTION

By imprisoning ourselves in sensual love, we are like a silkworm weaving its own cocoon. The wise are able to cut through and let go of the perceptions that lead to desires. Indifferent to the object of sensual love, they can avoid all suffering.

—Sutra on the Net of Sensual Love, Verse 17

The sutra uses the image of a silkworm winding the strands of a cocoon around itself so it can sleep. The silkworm creates its own cocoon. We make our own cocoon by choosing where to put our attention. There are different kinds of attention. There is the kind of attention that helps us, such as when we pay attention to our breathing or to the sound of the bell. That is called appropriate attention. The object of our attention determines whether we are peaceful or not. For example, when we're aware of the sound of the bell, our minds naturally settle down and become calm.

Feelings can be pleasant or unpleasant. When we see a form or hear a sound, we recognize it and we have a feeling and a perception about it. Our feeling leads to a perception. Perception follows and belongs with feeling. We think something is ugly or beautiful, pleasant or unpleasant. To have a pleasant sensation is to have a happy feeling; to have an unpleasant sensation is to have a feeling of suffering.

Often our perceptions are incorrect. We get in touch with an object and think that it embodies love, happiness, a self, or purity. We tend to think that love is something sentimental that will fill the emptiness inside us. We blame our suffering on another person or group, or on bad luck, but outside conditions are not the reason it appears. Our suffering was already there.

The birth of a human being is not a beginning but a continuation. When we're born, all the different kinds of seeds—seeds of goodness, cruelty, awakening—are already inside us. Whether the goodness or the cruelty in us is revealed depends on which seeds we cultivate by our actions and our ways of life. There are real painful feelings, strong emotions, and troubling perceptions that agitate us or make us afraid. With the energy of mindfulness, we can spend time with these difficult feelings without running away. We can embrace them the way a parent embraces a child, saying to them, "Darling, I am here for you; I have come back; I'm going to take care of you." In this way, we take care of our emotions, feelings, and perceptions.

APPEARANCE

Our mind dispersed, we tend to see the object of sensual love as something pure, ignorant that this growing attachment will remove all freedom and bring much suffering.
> —Sutra on the Net of Sensual Love, Verse 18

Those who are mindful are able to see the impure nature of the object of their sensual love. That is why they can let go of their desires, escape the jail, and avoid the misfortunes of old age and death.
> —Sutra on the Net of Sensual Love, Verse 19

As a culture, we place great stock in external appearance. Our attachment to physical beauty is something that we need to let go of, yet it seems that the majority of people are racing toward it. In the major cities of the world, you can see this clearly. Stores that sell cosmetics grow like mushrooms, full of products that promise to make us beautiful or fashionable. People go to doctors to change their bodies or faces. They rely on knives or chemicals to cut or adjust certain parts of their bodies, with the idea that this will somehow make them more attractive.

If we see an image and are seduced by it, it is because we don't know how to contemplate impermanence. Ignorant, we think that that form is wholesome and beautiful. We don't know that appearance doesn't contain anything real and long-lasting within it.

—Sutra on the Net of Sensual Love, Verse 16

Everyone wants their outer appearance to be more appealing, but there is nothing lasting or authentic about appearance. Still, we are seduced by our own reflection and the outer appearance of others. One thing we know for sure is that our appearance and bodily form will change, so there is no use being attached to it. There are hundreds of magazines and websites that tell us that in order to succeed, we have to look like this or that and use this or that kind of product. Many people suffer so much because they can't accept their bodies. They want to look different so they will be accepted.

Accepting your body is crucial for your peace and freedom. Every human being is born as a flower in the garden of humanity. And flowers differ from each other. If you can't accept your body and your mind, you can't be a home for yourself. Many young people don't accept who they are, and yet they want to be a home for someone else. But how can they be if they're not yet a home for themselves?

I've written a calligraphy that says, "Be beautiful; be yourself," which is a very important practice. When you practice building a home in yourself, you become more and more beautiful. You radiate your inner peace, warmth, and joy.

When our mind experiences pleasure, the five desires arise. The real hero quickly puts an end to these desires.
—Sutra on the Net of Sensual Love, Verse 29

When something is pleasant, lovely, and appealing, we're caught by it. But appealing appearances are deceptive. We get hooked by them and once we're caught, we suffer.

The Buddha once described someone who is very thirsty and sees a glass of fresh water. He thinks that if he drinks that water, he'll be satisfied. Looking closer, he sees there's a label saying the water is poison. If someone drinks it, that person will die. But the water looks so clear, fresh, and fragrant. A wise person would say "I'd better not drink that water. I'll find another source." But for many of us, the appearance is so appealing, we say, "I'll drink it. If I die, at least I'll die satisfied."

We have wisdom; we have understanding. We know that if we drink the poisonous water, we will die. But we drink it anyway. There are many of us like that, ready to die for something that seems very appealing. Yet there are so many sources that could satisfy our thirst without endangering us.

The Buddha gave another example, that of a fish swimming in a pond. The fish sees an appealing piece of bait, and when it's about to bite, another fish says, "No, don't do it; there's something inside that will hook you. I know because it happened to me." But the other fish is young, inexperienced, and full of energy. He says, "No! It's so appealing, I want to eat it. I'll survive like you did." The desire is so strong; We're willing to risk danger. Many young people say, "I want to feel good. I'll take responsibility, no matter what the consequences are." But while taking the bait might be pleasant for a few minutes, it will bring suffering soon enough.

SUFFERING

Sensual love inflicts us with suffering and ties us to worldly life. Worries and misfortunes caused by sensual love develop day and night like an invasive grass with tangled roots.

—Sutra on the Net of Sensual Love, Verse 2

The grass referred to in this verse is the grass used for thatching roofs. In the Pali text, it's called *dirana*. Its tangled roots are woven together, but its shoots look sweet and so people want to just pick the shoots. Underneath the earth, the grass grows very quickly and the roots become tangled in a mat. If we just water this grass and pick only the shoots, it continues its tangled growth. We need to dig up the roots completely so that the weed cannot come up again.

Most of us have tasted the suffering of sexual craving. We feel stuck in our relationship, in our work, and we think that satisfying our sensual desire will set us free. But it is this desire that is causing our worries and misfortunes. Worries and misfortunes are always there when we are ruled by sensual love. Even money and power will not protect us.

Most of us try to run away from our own suffering. We try to cover up the suffering inside and fill our feeling of emptiness by means of consumption. We consume food, music, or sex. Sometimes we drive or talk on the telephone in order to forget our suffering. The marketplace provides us with many ways to run away from ourselves. But running away doesn't help.

It takes courage to recognize what isn't working and to listen deeply to the suffering inside. We can use the energy of mindfulness, generated by breathing and walking, to get the strength and courage to go home to ourselves, recognize the suffering inside, and embrace it tenderly. We can listen deeply to our suffering and even respond to it, saying, "My suffering, I know you are there. I have come home, and I will take care of you."

There are times when we suffer and we don't know why. We don't know the nature of the suffering. That suffering may have been transmitted to us by our parents or our ancestors. They may not have been able to transform their suffering, and now they have transmitted it to us. First, we just acknowledge that it is there inside us. If we don't listen to our own suffering, we won't understand it, and we won't have compassion for ourselves. Compassion is the element that helps heal us. Only when we have compassion for ourselves, can we truly listen to another person.

So we embrace our pain, sorrow, and loneliness with the energy of mindfulness. The understanding and insight born from this practice will help transform the suffering inside us. We feel lighter; we begin to feel warmth and peace inside. That benefits us, and it benefits the other person as well. Then, when the other person joins you in building a home, you have an ally. You are helping him, and he is helping you.

WRONG VIEWS

> Those who are great and wise accomplish the way, liberating themselves from all attachment and suffering, emancipating themselves from all discrimination, and transcending all dualistic views.
>
> —Sutra on the Net of Sensual Love, Verse 22

The path of liberation is open to you; why would you take cords to bind yourself and others? The true teaching is that *this* lies in *that*; you cannot take this out of that. If a piece of driftwood is stuck on the side of the river, then it stops. It can't continue and will not reach the ocean. It doesn't matter on which side of the river you are stuck, you're still stuck. Moving through the center, not attached to any shore, is called taking the middle way.

According to the Buddha, there are four wrong views (*viparyasa*). Viparyasa means to turn upside down, or to reverse. All our suffering is caused by these four views that are contrary to the truth. The first wrong view is permanence (*nitya*). Things are impermanent (*anitya*) but we see them as permanent. The second wrong view is happiness (*sukha*).

Sometimes there is suffering (*dukkha*) but we think it is happiness. For example, we think drugs or alcohol make us happy, or when we're beginning an affair, we think it will bring us lasting happiness but instead it causes us and our loved ones to suffer.

The third wrong view is self (*atman*). People do not have a separate existence, just as a flower does not have a separate existence. The cloud is in the flower. The father is in the child. To see this truth is to see nonself. When we fully grasp nonself, we have no more attachment. When we're caught in dualistic thinking, in notions of this and that, then we see father and son as two different identities; we see body and consciousness, birth and death as two separate things.

The Buddha said, "Nothing is born or dies; Nothing is or is not; Nothing comes or goes". Birth and death, and coming and going, exist only in our mind. Scientists can see this truth, even if only intellectually. The French chemist Antoine Lavoisier said, "Nothing is lost; nothing is created;" everything is transformed.

When we observe a flower or a cloud, we can see there's no birth and no death, no coming and no going. Birth and death are simply the outward appearance of things. When we look more deeply we see that nothing is born and nothing dies. When we fully accept this, we'll have no more fear of what comes and goes. The Christian mystics touch this truth and express it as "resting in God." In Buddhism we call it "nirvana." If we want to arrive at nirvana, we must let go of our dualistic views of birth and death, coming and going, subject and object, and inside and outside. Our biggest obstacle is our dualistic view. Some people say that God is the creator and that the world is his creation. Seeing the creator and the creation as two separate things is a dualistic view.

The last wrong view is purity (*shuddhi*). We like to keep things separate, so we don't see the compost that helps make the garden, the mud that helps grow the lotus, or the dirt, sweat, and blood that help create a diamond. It's not pure but we think it is pure. This often happens when we go looking for an affair or a relationship. We think that because we find someone attractive, they have some kind of purity that is meaningful to us. But every person is made up of the pure and the impure, garbage as well as flowers.

When we are able to look deeply and let go of permanence, happiness, self, and purity, we arrive at insight. With this insight, instead of idealizing the object of our sensual desire, we can distinguish his or her true nature. We see that in essence he or she is impermanent, without a self, and impure—just like us.

SOVEREIGNTY

When the mind goes in the direction of sensual love, the tree of sexual love springs up and quickly sprouts buds. The mind becomes dispersed because the object of sensual love generates a violent fire in us. Those who look for sensual love are like monkeys jumping from branch to branch in search of fruits.
> —Sutra on the Net of Sensual Love, Verse 1

By tying ourselves up in the net of sensual love, or taking shelter under its umbrella, we bind ourselves to the cycle of attachment, like a fish swimming into his own trap.
> —Sutra on the Net of Sensual Love, Verse 20

Most of us live in environments where we have numerous opportunities to become busy and burdened. We go from event to event, from person to person, and the environment quickly pulls us away from mindfulness practice. We may have a girlfriend, a boyfriend, a partner, or a spouse, yet we still have unfulfilled sensual desires. It compels us to leave that person to follow another. The monkey swings from branch to branch in search of fruit. It eats one first, but it still craves another. Without delusion and craving, we wouldn't be caught by desire.

It's not other people who confine us; we confine ourselves. If we feel trapped, it's due to our own actions. No one is forcing us to tie ourselves up. We take the net of love and we wrap ourselves in it. We take the umbrella of love to cover ourselves up. We become like a fish going into the opening of a trap. There is a traditional Vietnamese bamboo trap with two openings. Going in is easy; going out is difficult.

At the moment of his awakening at the foot of the bodhi tree, the Buddha declared, "How strange—all beings possess the capacity to be awakened, to understand, to love, and to be free—yet they don't know it and they allow themselves to be carried away on the ocean of suffering." He saw that day and night we seek what is already there within us. We can call it Buddha nature or awakened nature, the true freedom that is the foundation of all peace and happiness. The capacity to be enlightened isn't something that someone else can offer to you. It's already there inside.

Each one of us is sovereign over the territory of our own being and the five elements we are made of: form (the body), feelings, perceptions, mental formations, and consciousness. Our practice is to look deeply into these five elements and discover the true nature of our being—the true nature of our suffering, our happiness, our peace, and our fearlessness.

But most of us have run away from our own territory and allowed conflicts and disorder to arise. We've been too afraid to go back to our territory and face the difficulties and suffering. Whenever we have fifteen "free" minutes, an hour or two, we have the habit of using our computers or cell phones, music, or conversations to forget and to run away from the reality of the elements that make up our beings. We think, "I'm suffering too much. I have too many problems. I don't want to go back to them anymore."

In order to claim our sovereign territory and transform the elements we are made of, we need to cultivate the energy of mindfulness. This is what will give us the strength to come back to ourselves. This energy is something real and concrete.

When we practice walking with awareness, our

solid peaceful steps cultivate the energy of mindfulness and bring us back to the present moment. When we sit and follow our breathing, aware of our in-breath and out-breath, we are cultivating the energy of mindfulness. When we have a meal in mindfulness, we invest all our being in the present moment and are aware of our food and of those who are eating with us. We can cultivate the energy of mindfulness, whatever we are doing—when we are working, or cleaning up, and even when we are being intimate with our loved one. Just a few days practicing like this can increase our energy of mindfulness, and that energy will help us, protect us, and give us courage to go back to ourselves, to see and embrace what is there in our territory.

Liberation and salvation can't come from anyone other than yourself. You can't wait for somebody to help you. You are your own island. Go back to your in-breath and out-breath. Touch the peace within you, and you can see more deeply. You'll see the root of the difficulty and you'll be able to undo the ties that bind you. Even if your mind is filled with the desire for sensual love, you'll be able to untie all these fetters.

CHAPTER 5

UNDERSTANDING
AND FORGIVENESS

> When we comprehend the Buddha's teachings, we
> see and understand the true nature of things without
> being caught by them.
>
> —Sutra on the Net of Sensual Love, Verse 24

WHEN WE UNDERSTAND OUR OWN suffering, it becomes much easier for us to understand another's.
Understanding is a gift. The other person may feel
understood for the first time. Understanding is the
other name of love. If you don't understand, you
can't love. If you don't understand your son, you can't
love him. If you don't understand your mother, you
can't love her. To offer understanding means to offer
love. Without understanding, the more we "love,"
the more we make ourselves and others suffer.

In Pearl Buck's novel *East Wind: West Wind*, a
young man leaves China to go to the United States
to become a doctor. The woman to whom he's
betrothed stays behind. She had always been educated
in the traditional Chinese way, including having her
feet bound and learning traditional ways to serve and
please a husband. By the time the young man had
finished his studies and returned to China to marry,
he'd been influenced by his time in the West. He

wanted his wife to express her own thoughts and not be afraid of, or subservient to him. But this was too difficult for her. It went against everything she'd learned about how to be a good wife. The couple spent many months estranged from one another, unable to achieve any real emotional or spiritual intimacy. The husband declined to be physically intimate with her while the chasm between them was so wide. Eventually they come to understand and love each other, and find happiness as a couple.

There are times you may sit and look at a child when she's sleeping. While the child sleeps, she reveals tenderness, suffering, and hope. Just contemplate a child sleeping and observe your feelings. Understanding and compassion will arise in you, and you will know how to take care of that child and make her happy. The same is true for your partner. You should have a chance to observe him when he sleeps. Look deeply, and see the tenderness that is revealed, the suffering, the hope, the despair that can be expressed during sleep. Sit there for fifteen minutes or half an hour, and just look. Understanding and compassion will arise in you, and you will know how to be there for your partner.

Our parents brought us into the world. If our

parents understood and loved each other, it gave us a chance to learn what true love is. If our parents didn't love and understand each other, we didn't have that chance. If our parents loved and understood each other, they became our first teachers in how to love. They didn't give us a course or classes. Their manner of taking care of each other was the best course.

The most precious inheritance parents can leave their children is their own happiness. Parents' happiness is the most valuable gift they can give their children. Your children can use those lessons the whole of their lives. You may not be able to leave them money, houses, and land, but you can help them be happy people. If we have happy parents, we have received the richest inheritance of all.

When a couple lives together, they have a tendency to think that they understand the other person completely, inside and out. They believe that they're not hiding anything from each other. They think that they completely know each other's body and mind. But, in reality, a human being is a universe to discover. What we see is often just the shell; the truth isn't easy to know.

Understanding another person isn't possible until we have practiced looking deeply at ourselves. Then, when we look at the other person, we'll begin to understand their suffering, because we've already seen and transformed our own. Once we can understand our loved one's suffering, we can help him or her. We will no longer reproach or blame the other person, because we'll have understanding in our hearts. Our way of looking at the other person will contain compassion. And the other person will be able to tell. Even if we haven't done or said anything, our way of looking already begins the process of healing.

If a couple doesn't practice mindfulness and does not try to understand their own and each other's suffering, they won't go far. They may continue to live together for a long time even when they're not happy. They may stay together for the sake of the children, or because they don't want to complicate their lives. There are many couples like that—they're together but they're not happy. There are other couples who can't support being in such a situation and so they separate or divorce.

Loneliness can only be healed by understanding and love. Sometimes we think that if we have sexual relations with someone else, we'll feel less lonely. But the truth is that such sex doesn't relieve the feeling of loneliness; it makes it worse. Sexuality should be accompanied by understanding and love. Without understanding and love, sex is empty.

DEEP LISTENING

Deep listening is necessary in order to truly be there for the person we love. In the person we love, there is suffering we haven't yet been able to see. Someone who can understand our suffering is our best friend. We want to be someone who can understand the suffering of others. To understand, we must listen deeply.

We could ask our partner, "Darling, I'd like it if you would speak to me of your childhood. What did you like to eat? What games did you play? What difficulties did you have?" If we're truly curious, we'll want to know and understand these things. When there is the curiosity and the desire to truly be there for the other person, she will tell us about her childhood. Simply by really listening to her about her early years—maybe she was happy, maybe she was tortured, and her suffering is still there after so many years, and nobody knew—we become her best friend.

"Let's listen to each other." "Let's be there for each other." We need to say these simple things. Otherwise, the union of two bodies becomes very monotonous after a time. Even when we're with our partner, we continue to have the feeling of being alone. So we look for another person to be with. In this way, we're always seeking. But don't believe that you see all that's contained in the depths of someone's eyes. If you have the impression that you know your beloved inside and outside, and that's why you're bored or restless, you're wrong. Are you sure that you know yourself?

In Asia there's a saying: "There are those who sleep in the same bed but who have different dreams." Once we have the capacity to love and understand, we can bring happiness to ourselves and to others. When we ask our beloved about his childhood he may answer, "The past is no longer part of my life; I don't want to talk about it." But if he isn't able to understand himself, he won't be able to understand others.

It seems simple to say that love is made of understanding but it is difficult to practice. We start with understanding our own suffering and discovering what causes our own craving. This helps us to transform and to not reproach or hate any longer. With understanding, we can love, and we can finally remove this feeling of loneliness in ourselves.

FORGIVENESS

Don't wait until it's too late to see what really matters to you. Because sensual desire can feel so overwhelming, it is often not until later that you see what havoc it has wreaked. Everybody makes mistakes, but you can't keep asking people to forgive you again and again. For example, instead of just saying, "I'm sorry I shouted at you," you need to train yourself not to shout so often. Make a commitment to take the time and practice seeing the roots of your behavior. Then you can make a real vow to transform yourself, to transform the situation, and to help people.

True repentance makes you happy and makes the other person happy. Without it, trust will disappear and both of you will be less happy. Vow that you will be transformed and that you will try your best to go in the direction of the practice. Otherwise, the other person will lose trust in you; and slowly you'll lose trust in yourself; and your relationship will be less strong than in the past. Act in such a way that trust is strengthened every day. You don't need to say anything. The other person will know by the way you act that you're truly beginning anew. Even if the other person doesn't see it right away, don't quarrel or be afraid. Just practice well and steadily, and slowly the truth will be revealed and the relationship will improve.

It's important to practice right thinking. Right thinking means looking deeply in order to have more understanding and compassion. Whenever you find yourself judging your partner, go back to your in-breath and out-breath, and ask, "How can I see this differently? Can I look more deeply to better understand her suffering and her difficulties?"

When you understand your partner, you can more easily accept him and have more compassion. This compassion will already bring you some relief. Don't continue to be shocked by his speech and behavior. Often people think, "This is unacceptable, I have to correct him." When you've had this kind of shock, go back to your in-breath and out-breath right away. Go back to your peace and look more deeply to see how things are. You can do this in any situation and you can accept and enjoy that situation. Compassion doesn't mean that you have to love that person who's so difficult. But if you stop and look deeper, you'll see that person's difficulties. If you can accept him, then you can love him.

Everyone has his or her areas of unskillfulness.

When you see that your way is not helping, then wake yourself up and stop your unskillful thoughts and behavior. Shouting at someone is not the way to help. If you've already shouted, then realize that this is one of your unskillful behaviors. Go back to your in-breath and out-breath and say, "I have to repair this." Then go to the other person and apologize, and tell yourself that next time you'll try your best to remember beforehand and act differently.

If you want to be a hero, you need to be able to do the work of being sincere with your partner and commit to being peace right now. Even if you have a lot of anger, try to stop and look deeper to understand yourself and others. You have to use your faith in the practice and try to transform today. Don't wait until tomorrow.

CHAPTER 6

THREE KEYS
TO HAPPINESS

> If we want to be happy and joyful, then we must be determined to let go of attachment . . . The absence of attachment leads to true peace and joy.
>
> —Sutra on the Net of Sensual Love, Verse 5

WE TEND TO THINK THAT IN ORDER to be happy, we need certain outside conditions; we must have this or that before happiness can arrive. But happiness comes from our way of looking at things. We're not happy, but other people under the same conditions are happy. This verse reminds us to be like the lotus leaf. Drops of water glide off the lotus leaf without being absorbed by it. We aspire to be like this lotus leaf, so that our sensual desire glides off us and we keep our equanimity.

Our happiness depends on our insight. We may have had what we think of as a bad accident. But if we look more deeply, we may see that this accident might have a beneficial effect in making us more mindful in the future and helping us to avoid an even bigger accident. Sometimes it seems we're experiencing what we might call good luck. But, it's wise to be cautious, because good luck can bring a negative consequence in its wake.

When you're not happy, it's important to look deeply into the situation. If you say, "I'm not happy in this place or with this person," maybe that's not really true. If you're not happy, it's not because of the situation outside; it's because of you. You can be happy in any situation. This doesn't mean that you should be passive and accept things as they are. You accept, yes, in the sense that you see clearly how things are; you see the negative and you also see the positive.

Don't think that without this or that you can't be happy. Go ahead and try your best to have what you want, but in the meantime you can still be happy. For example, if you're waiting for a visa so you can leave the country, don't say, "I'll only be happy once I've got the visa." Perhaps when you arrive in the other country, you won't be happy there either. So you have to train yourself to think: "Even if I don't get the visa, it's okay. I'm happy here." That way if you're able to obtain the visa, you'll have the capacity to also accept the situation as it is in the other country.

RELEASING OUR COWS

There's an old story about the Buddha sitting with his monks. They had just finished eating their lunch together in mindfulness. Suddenly a farmer came by.

He was suffering so much. He said, "Dear brothers, have you seen my cows going by? I have five cows but for some reason this morning they all ran away. I also have two acres of sesame plants, and this year the insects ate all the sesame seeds. There's nothing left. I think I'm going to kill myself."

With compassion, the Buddha looked at him and said, "Dear friend, we've been sitting here for more than an hour and we haven't seen any cows. You might want to look for them in another direction."

When the farmer left, the Buddha turned around and looked at the monks sitting with him. He smiled and said, "My dear friends, you are very lucky because you don't have any cows."

The cows represent the things to which we are attached. So the practice is to learn how to release our cows. Sit down and breathe in and out in mindfulness and concentration, and identify your cows. Call your cows by their true names, and see whether you have the ability to release any of them. The more you release, the happier you become. Cow-releasing is an art, a practice. The idea you have about happiness is a cow, a strong one. It needs great insight and courage to let it go.

Suppose you want something very much. You

think that if you don't get that something, happiness won't be possible. You get caught in that idea. But, in reality, there are people who have that thing who are miserable, and there people who don't have that thing who are perfectly happy. You have an idea about happiness. If you haven't been able to be happy, it may be because of that idea. Release that idea, and happiness can come more easily. There are many doors to happiness. If you open all of them, then happiness has many ways to come to you. But if the situation is that you have closed all the doors except one, then that is why happiness cannot come. Perhaps happiness can't come through that one door. So don't close any of the doors. Open all the doors. Don't commit yourself to just one idea of happiness. Remove the idea of happiness that you have, and then happiness can come, this afternoon.

Many of us are caught in our ideas of how we can be truly happy. We are attached to a number of things that we think are crucial for our well-being. We may have suffered a lot because of our attachment to those things, but we don't have the courage to release them; it doesn't feel safe to do so. But it may be that we continue to suffer because of our attachment to those things. It may be a person, a material object, or a position in society, anything. We think that without that person or thing we will not be safe, and that is why we're caught by it.

Happiness depends first of all on having the deep desire for happiness, and then on having a spiritual path to follow. Every day, do some little thing on that path, and you will be happy. Don't try to do big things. Do small things to make yourself happier, to make your friends happier. When you cook a dish or clear the table, do it beautifully, for yourself and for the people around you. You can start right away.

There are three key practices that can transform your suffering and allow you to truly make a home for yourself so that you have solidity and understanding to give your partner. They also lead you to great joy. They are the practices of mindfulness (*smrti*), concentration (*samadhi*), and insight (*prajña*). With mindfulness, concentration, and insight, we can purify our mind so that the afflictions will be lighter, we can connect more deeply with our loved ones, and we can be free.

MINDFULNESS

Letting go, releasing, is one technique that can bring about joy and happiness. Mindfulness is another method that brings about joy and happiness. Suppose you are a young person. You can hike, jump, and run; you can do many things. You're full of energy. Being young is a wonderful thing. There are those of us who can't do those things anymore; we're too old now. So breathe in and feel yourself young and full of energy. "Breathing in, I know that I am still young." And that awareness brings happiness.

When I breathe in, I can focus my attention on my eyes, and the insight comes that my eyes are still good enough; my eyes are still in good condition. "Breathing in, I'm aware of my eyes. Breathing out I smile to my eyes." To some people this may seem silly at first; but this way of practicing mindfulness can bring insight and happiness. It's wonderful to have eyes still in good condition. You need only to open your eyes in order to enter into a paradise of forms and colors. Spring is here; there is a paradise there. And because you have eyes in good condition, you can enter the paradise easily. You don't have to make any effort; just open your eyes.

For those of us who have lost our eyesight, this paradise is no longer available through our eyes. Our deepest wish is to recover our eyesight in order to see paradise again. But those of us who still have eyes in good condition can say, "Breathing in, I am aware of my eyes; Breathing out, I know they are in good condition." And the insight comes that you have a condition of happiness that is already there. That is mindfulness, and mindfulness brings joy and happiness. Mindfulness tells you that you are still young. Mindfulness tells you that your eyes are in good condition.

"Breathing in, I'm aware of my heart." You recognize your heart and you know that your heart still functions normally. It's wonderful to have a heart that functions normally. Those of us who don't have a heart like that are fearful of having a heart attack at any time. So every time we're mindful of our heart functioning normally, we feel happy. With mindfulness, happiness comes just like that, in one second. Mindfulness helps us recognize the many conditions of happiness that are inside us and around us.

So we have to train ourselves to learn that mindfulness is a source of happiness. We don't need money; we don't have to go shopping. We just need mindfulness. First we develop the capacity of letting go. Then we develop the capacity of being mindful. Then we can see that happiness is already available.

Some of us have so many conditions for

happiness, yet we're not happy. Other people envy us and imagine we're happy people. We have so many conditions of happiness, yet we don't recognize and treasure them.

CONCENTRATION

When we're mindful of something, we can absorb it and concentrate on it. Such concentration increases the quality of our happiness. Suppose you have a cup of tea. When you're mindful and concentrated, your tea becomes something very real and the time of tea-drinking makes you so happy. Your mind is not disturbed. It's not dwelling in the past, in the future, or on your current projects. Your mind is focused entirely on the tea. That's concentration. Tea is the object of your concentration. So drinking tea in that moment can make you very happy; and the more you are concentrated, the happier you become. Contemplating a beautiful sunrise, you're not distracted by thinking about the past or the future. The more concentrated you become, the more you see the beauty all arond you. So concentration is a source of happiness.

INSIGHT

Insight always liberates you. If you're inhabited by fear, worries, desire, or craving, you can't be peaceful. But when you have insight, fear and craving are removed; you are free; and true joy and happiness come to you. The practice of meditation—releasing, mindfulness, concentration, and insight—is the practice of true love.

CHAPTER 7

THE FOUR ELEMENTS OF TRUE LOVE

TRUE LOVE MAKES US HAPPY. If love doesn't make us happy, it's not love; it's something else.

The word love has so many meanings. We say we love ice cream, a pair of jeans, or a certain movie. We have abused that word and have to heal it. Words can get sick and lose their meaning. We have to detoxify the words and make them healthy again.

True love is made of loving kindness (*maitri*), compassion (*karuna*), joy (*mudita*), and equanimity (*upeksha*). True love brings joy and peace, and relieves suffering. You don't need another person in order to practice love. Practice love on yourself. When you succeed, loving another person becomes very natural. Your love will be like a lamp that shines; it will make many, many people happy.

The holy spirit is made of mindfulness, concentration, and insight. When you practice the four qualities of true love, your love is healing and transformative, and it has the element of holiness in. Then sexual intimacy becomes something very beautiful. Love is a wonderful thing. It gives us the ability to offer joy and happiness, relieve suffering, and transcend all kinds of separation and barriers.

LOVING KINDNESS

Maitri, loving kindness, is the first element of love. The word maitri comes from the Sanskrit word *mitra*, which means friend. So love is friendship, and that friendship should bring about happiness. Otherwise, what's the use of friendship? To be a friend means to offer happiness. If love doesn't offer happiness, if it makes the other person cry all the time, then it's not love; it's not maitri; it's the opposite.

Maitri is translated into English as "loving kindness," the ability to offer happiness. True love requires this element. Love does not just mean love for another person. Self-love is the foundation for loving another person. If you don't know how to love and offer happiness to yourself, how can you love and offer happiness to another person? If you don't know anything about happiness, how can you offer it? Live in a way that brings you joy and happiness, and then you'll be able to offer it to another person.

We know that happiness has something to do with suffering. If we don't understand suffering, we can't know what happiness is. Understanding suffering is the very foundation of happiness. If you don't know how to handle a painful feeling in you, how can you help another person to do so? So self-love is crucial for loving another person. A successful relationship depends on us recognizing our own painful feelings and emotions inside—not fighting them, but accepting, embracing, and transforming them to get relief.

COMPASSION

The second element of love is karuna, which is translated into English as "compassion." Karuna is the capacity to relieve suffering—to remove and transform suffering. When someone you love suffers, you're motivated to do something to help. But if you don't know how to handle the suffering in yourself, how can you help the other person to handle his suffering? We first have to handle the suffering in ourselves. Whenever a painful feeling or emotion arises, we should be able to be present with it—not fight it, but recognize it.

We can learn how to embrace and accept suffering and use mindfulness, concentration, and insight to understand its nature. Then we get relief. The Buddha's teaching is very clear and concrete. He doesn't just say we have to love, but he tells us how to love. He doesn't just say we can transform our suffering; he tells us exactly how—step by step.

We need to not only recognize the suffering, pain, and difficulties within us, we need to devote time to dealing with them and transforming them. Using mindfulness and concentration, we can nurture our own feelings of joy and happiness. If we know the art of releasing, the art of mindfulness, concentration, and insight, then we can bring in feelings of joy and happiness at any time.

The word "compassion" does not quite reflect the true meaning of karuna. The prefix "com" means "together" and "passion" means "to suffer." So to be compassionate means to suffer together with the other person. But karuna doesn't require suffering. Karuna is the capacity to relieve suffering. It's the capacity to relieve the suffering in you and in the other person. When you know the practice of mindful breathing; of tenderly holding your pain and sorrow; of looking deeply into the nature of suffering; then you can transform that suffering and bring relief. You don't have to suffer, and you don't have to suffer with the other person. Both of you can practice this way.

Suppose you're a compassionate physician. When a patient comes in complaining of pain and fear, even as a good doctor, you don't have to suffer with that person in order to be kind to him.

We have to distinguish between the willingness to love and the capacity to love. You may be motivated by the willingness to love, but if that is your only motivation, the other person will suffer. So the willingness to love is not yet love. Many parents love their children. Yet they make them suffer a lot in the name of love. They're often not capable of understanding their children's suffering, difficulties, hopes, and aspirations. We have to ask ourselves, "Am I really loving the other person by understanding them or am I just projecting my own needs?"

Love doesn't just mean the intention or willingness to make someone happy, but the capacity to do so. That capacity to love is something you have to learn and cultivate. Look into yourself and recognize the suffering in yourself. If you recognize, embrace, and transform your suffering and difficulties, then you are loving yourself. Based on that experience, you will succeed in helping another person to do the same, bringing a feeling of joy and happiness.

JOY

Joy, mudita, is the third element of true love. Love should bring us joy. If love brings only tears, why should we love? If you provide yourself with joy, you'll know how to bring joy to your partner and to the world.

Mudita has been translated as sympathetic or altruistic joy. I don't like that translation because if you don't have joy, you can't offer joy. Joy is for you, but it is also for me. A true practitioner knows how to bring joy to himself. We don't need to talk about altruistic joy. Joy is just joy. If you are really joyful and your joy is healthy, then that benefits other people. If you're not joyful, not fresh, or not smiling, then that doesn't benefit anyone. If you're inhabited by joy and freshness, even if you do nothing, we profit from you.

EQUANIMITY

The fourth element of true love is upeksha, meaning equanimity and nondiscrimination. This is the foundation of true love. In true love, there is no distinction between the one who loves and the one who is loved. Your suffering is my own suffering. My happiness is your happiness. Lover and beloved are one. There's no longer any barrier. True love has this element of the abolishing of self. Happiness is no longer an individual matter. Suffering is also no longer an individual matter. There's no distinction between us.

Another way to translate upeksha is inclusiveness. In true love, you don't exclude anyone. If your love is true love, it will benefit not only humans, but also animals, plants, and minerals. When you love one person, it's an opportunity for you to love everyone, all beings. Then you are going in a good direction, and that is true love. But if you love someone and you get caught up in suffering and attachment, then you get cut off from others. That's not true love.

The deepest gift mindfulness can bring us is the wisdom of nondiscrimination. We are not noble by birth. We are noble only by virtue of the way we think, speak, and act. The person who practices true love has the wisdom of nondiscrimination, and it informs all of his or her actions. You don't discriminate between yourself, your partner, all people, and all living beings. Your heart has grown large and your love knows no obstacles.

Cultivating the four elements of true love—loving kindness, compassion, joy, and equanimity—is the secret to nourishing deep and healthy relationships. When you practice with these elements regularly, you can handle the difficulties in your relationships and transform the suffering you feel inside. You become like a Buddha. You love everyone and every species. Your presence in the world becomes very important, because your presence is the presence of love.

CHAPTER 8

OUR TRUE
VOW

> Don't keep company with those who go against the true teachings. Don't let yourself be pulled along the path of attachment. If the practitioner has not yet transcended time, he is still caught in dualistic views.
> —Sutra on the Net of Sensual Love, Verse 23

THE SUTRA FOCUSES ON SENSUAL love and sexual desire, but its teaching applies to desire for power, fame, money, and good food, as well as sex. We know that if we eat a certain food, it will upset our digestion, but we still eat it. The way out is to beware of the superficial appearance. From outside, something may look very pleasant. But we have to look deeper and use that deep understanding to see the superficial aspects of the object of our desire. Our understanding can overcome our cravings.

When our senses come in contact with something, we pay attention to it. Naturally, we assign a feeling or a judgment to what we're paying attention to and experience it as pleasant, unpleasant, or neutral. That feeling brings about a perception. When we see something as unpleasant, we want to reject it. When we see something as pleasant, then we want to grasp it.

Our deepest desire, what motivates us and determines the direction our actions will take, is called volition or aspiration. It can be positive or negative. This is the energy that keeps us alive. We want to to do something with our lives. If we're motivated by compassion and true love, we have a wholesome volition. But if our desire is pushing us into negative environments and situations that don't bring us more joy and compassion, then instead of nourishing us, our volition is harming us.

In sensual love, volition can look like a kind of sickness called "lovesickness." We are addicted to the shadow of a figure, and we cannot forget him or her. When we are caught in the net of sensual desire, all our longings and our perceptions are dyed the color of sensual love. When walking we think about it; when sitting we think about it. Watching the moon we also remember it; watching a cloud we remember it again. The mind of sensual desire is a current; it's not a block or a clod of earth. The current sweeps our thoughts, perceptions, and everyday actions along with it.

DEEP ASPIRATION

What is our aspiration? Is it awakening, mindfulness, or the relief of suffering? Do we really want to realize our greatest aspiration? If we truly want to accomplish our aspirations, then why would we go along a path that goes against them, and leaves us without enough energy to practice and help ourselves and others?

The bodhisattva Kshitigarbha, who embodies this strong aspiration, made this vow: "Wherever there is suffering, I vow to go there and help; I feel fulfillment, contentment, and happiness helping people." Having a deep aspiration helps others and brings you fulfillment and contentment at the same time. If you and your partner both have a deep aspiration, then not only will you support each other's happiness, you will bring more happiness to the world in ways that you, by yourself, cannot.

When your aspiration is to fill yourself with great mindfulness and love, that aspiration is called *bodhicitta*, beginner's mind, the mind of love. It is the desire to help relieve the suffering of others and help others to become awakened. We should live in such a way that this aspiration becomes more solid every day. If our aspiration erodes and weakens, we will not succeed on our path of practice. We need to practice mindfulness daily in order to fulfill our aspiration. We need to patiently pursue our aspiration, but we don't lose the present moment—we enjoy the present moment and we use it to realize our deepest desire.

Our deep aspiration is an immense source of energy. Without an aspiration we wither and lose our vitality. We need to observe that source of vitality within us. Is it great enough? If there's not enough energy, then we're not yet solid. A storm can still knock us down.

Inside each of us is a great being, someone peaceful, full of light, understanding, and compassion. This person carries a sword of understanding that cuts through the bonds of suffering. With great understanding, we see the way out of our bondage. We discover the lightness and compassion necessary to love someone else. We can awaken this great person within and realize our true aspiration, without distraction or interference.

When you and your partner share an aspiration and a practice, there is no place for jealousy, because you're both faithful to the same aspiration. Whatever the other person does, you do it with him. You share everything. That is the spirit of upeksha. It makes fidelity possible.

Of course you still have your freedom, and your partner still has her freedom intact. Love is not a kind of prison. True love gives us a lot of space. Because you are connected spiritually and emotionally as well as physically, you do not need to always be in the same place or doing the same thing. You do not worry if your beloved is over here today and you are over there.

AWAKENING TO THE BUDDHA WITHIN

The name "Buddha" means "one who is awake." When Siddhartha woke up to the reality of the world all around him and made his vow to live fully in each moment, he was thirty-five years old. At thirty-five most of us still have a lot of sexual energy. In Plum Village we have many young monks and nuns who have sexual energy like everyone else. But they practice channeling that energy toward their great aspiration and are not manipulated by it. We can even use sexual energy to support us on the spiritual path. Digging up the root of sensual love doesn't mean we eliminate our sexual energy. Instead insight and compassion allow us to handle our sexual energy with skill.

Awakening is a matter of insight. Once we have insight, although we still have the energy of sexual desire, we can manage it easily. The sutra talks about uprooting the energy of sexual desire. This doesn't mean we harshly cut this down or completely eliminate it. When restless sexual desire arises, we pay attention to it with enough understanding and enough love that it dissipates and does not grow.

FULL-TIME BUDDHA

When you begin to practice mindfulness, you begin as a part-time Buddha. Slowly you become a full-time Buddha. Sometimes you are a Buddha; sometimes you fall back; and then, with steady practice, you become a Buddha once again. Buddhahood is within reach because, like the Buddha, you're a human being. You can become a Buddha whenever you like. Buddha is available in the here and now, anytime, anywhere.

When you are a part-time Buddha, your romantic relationships may go well some of the time. When you are a full-time Buddha, you can find a way to be present and happy in your relationship full-time, no matter what difficulties arise.

Becoming a Buddha is not so difficult. A Buddha is someone who is enlightened, capable of loving and forgiving. You know that at times you're like that. So enjoy being a Buddha when you can. When you sit, allow the Buddha in you to sit. When you walk, allow the Buddha in you to walk. Enjoy your practice. If you don't become a Buddha, who will?

To become a Buddha, we have to do three things. We have to untangle the cords of sensual desire, commit to our deep aspiration, and free ourselves from dualistic thinking.

Every single person contains the seeds of goodness, kindness, and enlightenment. We all have the seeds of Buddha nature within us. To give the Buddha a chance to manifest, we have to water those seeds. When we act as if people have these seeds inside them, it gives us and them the strength and energy to help these seeds grow and flower. When we behave as if we don't believe in our inherent goodness and that of others, then we blame ourselves and others for our suffering and we lose our happiness.

You can use the goodness in yourself to transform your suffering and the tendency to be angry, cruel, and afraid. But don't throw your suffering away. Use it. Your suffering is the compost that gives you the understanding to nourish your happiness and the happiness of your loved ones.

CHAPTER 9

FIDELITY

Leaving desires behind, not heeding the tracks of love's passage, we tear apart the net of love; nothing can harm us anymore.

—Sutra on the Net of Sensual Love, Verse 21

TO COMMIT TO ANOTHER PERSON is to embark on a very adventurous journey. There is no one "right person" who will make it easier. You must be very wise and very patient to keep your love alive so it will last for a long time.

The first year of a committed relationship already reveals how difficult it is. When you first commit to someone, you have a beautiful image of them, and you commit to that image rather than the person. When you live with the person twenty-four hours a day, you begin to discover the reality of the other person doesn't quite correspond with the image you have of him or her. Sometimes you're disappointed.

In the beginning of a relationship, you're very passionate. But that passion may only last a short time—maybe six months, a year, or two years. Then, if you're not skillful, if you don't practice mindfulness, concentration, and insight, suffering will be born in you and in the other person. When you see someone else, you might think you'd be happier with them. In Vietnam, there is a saying: "Standing on top of one mountain and gazing at the top of another, you think you'd rather be standing on the other mountain."

When we commit to a partner, either in a marriage ceremony or in a private way, usually it is because we believe we can be and want to be faithful to our partner for the whole of our lives. That is a challenge that requires consistent strong practice. Many of us don't have any models of loyalty and faithfulness around us. The U.S. divorce rate is around fifty percent, and for nonmarried but committed partners, the rates are similar or higher.

We tend to compare ourselves with others and wonder if we have enough to offer in a relationship. Many of us feel unworthy. We're thirsty for truth, goodness, compassion, spiritual beauty, and we're sure these things don't exist within us, so we go looking outside. Sometimes we think we've found the ideal partner who embodies all that is good, beautiful, and true. That person may be a romantic partner, a friend, or a spiritual teacher. We see all the good in that person and we fall in love. After a time, we usually discover that we've had a wrong perception of that person, and we become disappointed.

Beauty and goodness are there in each of us. A true spiritual partner is one who encourages you to look deep inside yourself for the beauty and love you've been seeking. A true teacher is someone who helps you discover the teacher in yourself.

PUTTING DOWN DEEP ROOTS

To keep our commitment to our partner and to weather the most difficult storms, we need strong roots. If we wait until there is trouble with our partner to try and solve it, we won't have built strong enough roots to withstand the assault. Often we think we're balanced when, in reality, that balance is fragile. We only need a wind to blow on the tips of our branches for us to fall down. A juniper tree has its roots planted deep in the heart of the earth. As a result it is solid and strong. There are some trees that appear to be quite steady, but they only need one raging storm to knock them down. Resilient trees remain truly steady in a violent storm because their roots are deep.

THE FIRST ROOT: FAITH

We think that when we commit to another person, we need to have faith in that person, to trust that they are worthy of our commitment. But really, the other person is someone with challenges and strengths, just like everyone else. If we place our faith in a god, then perhaps later we will lose that faith. If we have faith in a person, then we may also lose faith in that person. We should have faith in something more steadfast and enduring. We need to have faith in ourselves and the Buddha within.

When we see people who have the capacity to generate happiness, this gives us faith in our own Buddha nature. This faith is not a theory; it is a reality. We can look around and see that a person who lives with happiness and compassion has the capacity to make others happy. Someone who does not have the capacity to understand and love suffers and causes others to suffer.

In the Kalama Sutra, there's a passage where a young person says to the Buddha, "There are many spiritual teachers who visit us. Many of them also say that their way is the true way, and that we should follow them. We don't know whom we should follow! Please, Buddha, teach us what we should do."

The Buddha said, "Do not have faith in something because a famous spiritual teacher said it. Do not have faith in something because it was recorded in scriptures. Do not have faith in something because everyone believes in it. Do not have faith in something because it is laid down in custom. Hearing something, we should examine it closely, comprehend it, and apply it. If, when we apply it, there is a result, then we can have faith in it. If there is no result, then we should not have faith in it just because of custom, scripture, or some spiritual teacher."

THE SECOND ROOT: PRACTICE

No matter how much we want to commit to a healthy relationship, there are so many external messages teaching us to go after our cravings. We are full of so many old habits. If we don't practice mindfulness, our cravings and sensual desires will overwhelm us. Happiness is made up of our mindfulness, concentration, and insight. Each time we practice sitting meditation, walking meditation, awareness of breathing, loving speech, deep listening, or any other mindfulness practice, our roots are growing stronger and deeper and we are gaining more solidity and strength.

If we practice conscious breathing, we will calm the turmoil and sorrow in our minds whenever they appear. If at first our practice is not successful, we continue until we see the results. When we see that the practice works, slowly our faith in it grows. Our faith is always based on empirical evidence. We do not believe it just because it has been repeated many times by others.

THE THIRD ROOT:
COMMUNITY SUPPORT

In a relationship in which you and your partner share the same kind of aspirations, then you become one, and together you become an instrument of love and peace. Whatever you do, you do together, because you are a community, a Sangha of two people, of three or four people, or of one hundred people who have faith in the same thing: that we have the capacity to understand better, to love better, and to have more happiness.

After his enlightenment, the first thing the Buddha did was to look for fellow practitioners so he could build a Sangha. We can't find happiness unless we have a refuge. I live in a community of monks, nuns, and laypeople at the Plum Village Meditation Practice Center in southwest France. My community is my true home. Even if you are just two people, if you nourish each other's joy and mindfulness, then you have a Sangha, a mindful community. If your family only has two people, that is the smallest Sangha. If you have a child, you have three Sangha members. If you live with more people, you have a Sangha of four, or five, or more. Your family is your home, your refuge.

With our faith in our community of two or more, we can go anywhere. The Sangha is like the earth. It can absorb so much and can hold such deep roots. These roots reach down into the whole community. When our roots reach down deeply into the Sangha, our roots begin to draw nutrients from the Sangha body to increase our own strength and keep us standing upright.

When the three roots of faith, practice, and community support have fed us deeply, then we will be solid both alone and in our relationships. We will not just survive; we will flourish. No violent storm can throw us. Often in our daily lives, we are just focused on survival. But fidelity is not a question of survival. It is one of vitality.

TWO GARDENS

You have two gardens: your own garden and that of your beloved. First, you have to take care of your own garden and master the art of gardening. In each one of us there are flowers and garbage. The garbage is the anger, fear, discrimination, and jealousy within us. If you water the garbage, you will strengthen the negative seeds. If you water the flowers of compassion, understanding, and love, you will strengthen the positive seeds. What you grow is up to you.

If you don't know how to practice selective watering in your own garden, then you won't have enough wisdom to help water the flowers in the garden of your beloved. In cultivating your own garden well, you also help to cultivate her garden.

Even a week of practice can make a big difference. You can do it. Every time you practice walking mindfully, investing your mind and body in every step, you are taking your situation in hand. Every time you breathe in and know you are breathing in, every time you breathe out and smile to your outbreath, you are yourself, you are your own master, and you are the gardener in your own garden. We are relying on you to take good care of your garden, so that you can help your beloved to take care of hers.

If you have a difficult relationship, and you want to make peace with the other person, you have to go home to yourself. Go home to your garden and cultivate the flowers of peace, compassion, understanding, and joy. Only after that can you come to your partner and be patient and compassionate.

When we commit to another person, we make a promise to grow together, sharing the fruit and progress of practice. It is our responsibility to take care of each other. Every time the other person does something in the direction of change and growth, we should show our appreciation.

If you have been together with your partner for some years, you may have the impression that you know everything about this person. But that isn't true. Scientists can study a speck of dust for years, and they still don't claim to understand everything about it. If a speck of dust is that complex, how can you know everything about another person? Your partner needs your attention and your watering of his or her positive seeds. Without that attention, your relationship will wither.

We have to learn the art of creating happiness. If during your childhood, you saw your parents do things that created happiness in the family, you already know what to do. But many of us didn't have these role models. The problem is not one of being wrong or right, but one of being more or less skillful. Living together is an art. Even with a lot of goodwill, we can still make the other person very unhappy. Mindfulness is the paintbrush in the art of happiness. When we are mindful, we are more artful and happiness blooms.

OUR TRUE HOME

We're all searching for a place where we feel safe and comfortable, a home where we can be truly ourselves. As we become more skilled in mindfulness and lay down the roots of fidelity, we can truly relax with our partner. All the restlessness and searching inside dissipates when we find our true home.

Our true home is inside. When we look deeply and honestly at our own suffering, energies, and views, we find a peace that comes from being comfortable in our own bodies. But our true home is not only inside us. Once we have become comfortable in ourselves, then we can begin listening deeply to the suffering of our loved ones, and begin understanding their experiences and views. Then we can become a true home for each other. In Vietnam, each person in a married couple calls the other "my home." When a man is asked, "Where is your wife?" he may answer, "My home is at the Post Office." If someone asks a woman where she got something, she might say, "My home made it." When a husband calls his wife, he asks, "My home?" And she answers, "Here I am."

If we're practicing mindfulness, there doesn't have to be a conflict between the true home inside us and the true home we make with our partner. There is no discrimination, no craving. In our true home together there is only relaxation, liberation, and joy.

SUTRA ON THE
NET OF
SENSUAL LOVE

1   When the mind goes in the direction of sensual love, the tree of sexual love springs up and quickly sprouts buds. The mind becomes dispersed because the object of sensual love generates a violent fire in us. Those who look for sensual love are like monkeys jumping from branch to branch in search of fruits.

2   Sensual love inflicts us with suffering and ties us to worldly life. Worries and misfortunes caused by sensual love develop day and night like an invasive grass with tangled roots.

3   Blinded by attachment, sooner or later we fall into sensual love. Anxiety mounts day by day, just as water fills a pond drop by drop.

4   In life there are many worries and sorrows, but there's no greater sorrow than that brought by sensual love. Only when a practitioner can let go of sensual love can he release all worry.

5   If we want to be happy and joyful, then we must be determined to let go of attachment. Free from attachment, we are no longer caught in the circle of samsara—not burdened by anxiety nor restlessly searching for what is unwholesome. The absence of attachment leads to true peace and joy.

6   If we have been deeply caught in love, then, on our deathbed, surrounded by relatives, we will see just how long is the path of worry and suffering that lies before us. The suffering caused by love often leads to risky situations and numerous disasters.

7   Practitioners should not go in the direction of sensual love. We must start by finding a way to wholly uproot the tree of sensual love so its roots can no longer sprout; it's not like simply cutting reeds above ground.

8   The roots of sensual love are deep and firm. The tree may be cut, yet the branches and leaves sprout again. If sensual love is not uprooted, the suffering it causes will return.

9 Just as a monkey jumps from one tree to another, so people jump from one prison of sensual love to another.

10 The mind of sensual love is like a stream of water following the course of habit energy and pride. Our thoughts and perceptions become tainted by the hues of sensual love; we hide the truth from ourselves and cannot see it.

11 The stream of the mind continues to flow freely, allowing the knots of sensual love to burgeon and snag. Only real insight is capable of discerning this reality clearly, helping us to cut through its roots in our mind.

12 The stream of sensual love permeates our thoughts and perceptions, growing stronger and entwining itself with them. Its source is bottomless; with it, old age and death advance quickly.

13 The branches of the tree of sensual love continue to grow, nourished by these nutriments, building up a mound of hatred and resentment. Those who have little insight hasten in that direction.

14 The wise do not consider the chains and shackles of jail to be the toughest restraints. The chains of attachment are the strongest of the ties that bind.

15 The wise know that sensual love is the most confining jail of all; escape from it is difficult. They know that only by putting an end to sensual love can they really be at peace.

16 If we see an image and are seduced by it, it is because we don't know how to contemplate impermanence. Ignorant, we think that form is wholesome and beautiful. We don't know that appearance doesn't contain anything real and long-lasting within it.

17 By imprisoning ourselves in sensual love, we are like a silkworm weaving its own cocoon. The wise are able to cut through and let go of the perceptions that lead to desires. Indifferent to the object of sensual love, they can avoid all suffering.

18 Our mind dispersed, we tend to see the object of sensual love as something pure, ignorant that this growing attachment will remove all freedom and bring much suffering.

19 Those who are mindful are able to see the impure nature of the object of their sensual love. That is why they can let go of their desires, escape the jail, and avoid the misfortunes of old age and death.

20 By tying ourselves up in the net of sensual love, or taking shelter under its umbrella, we bind ourselves to the cycle of attachment, like a fish swimming into his own trap. Caught by old age and death, we long for the object of our love, like a calf seeking his mother's udder.

21 Leaving desires behind, not heeding the tracks of love's passage, we tear apart the net of love; nothing can harm us anymore.

22 Those who are great and wise accomplish the way, liberating themselves from all attachment and suffering, emancipating themselves from all discrimination, and transcending all dualistic views.

23 Don't keep company with those who go against the true teachings. Don't let yourself be pulled along the path of attachment. If the practitioner has not yet transcended time, he is still caught in dualistic views.

24 When we comprehend the Buddha's teachings, we see and understand the true nature of things without being caught by them. We know, then, how to break the ties of sensual love in our minds.

25 To offer the authentic teaching is the most precious gift of all. The scent of ethics is the most fragrant. Living according to an authentic teaching is the greatest happiness. Putting an end to sensual love is the definitive victory over suffering.

26 Those with little understanding often tie themselves up with the rope of sensual desire. They don't yet want to cross to the other shore. Greed creates corruption and brings great misfortune to them and to others.

27 The greedy mind is like the earth; greed, anger, and ignorance, the seeds. The happiness reaped by those capable of offering and serving is immeasurable.

28 With few companions but abundant goods, the merchant becomes anxious and fearful. The wise don't run after desires. They know that love for sensual pleasures is an enemy that can ruin their lives.

29 When our mind experiences pleasure, the five desires arise. The real hero quickly puts an end to these desires.

30 When desire stops, there is no more fear. We are then truly free, peaceful, and happy. When the practitioner has no more desire, nor any internal formations, he has freed himself from the abyss.

31 My dear sensual desire, I know your source. The desiring mind comes from wants and wrong perceptions. Now I have no more wants and wrong perceptions about you, so how can you arise?

32 If we don't cut down the tree of sensual love at its roots, it will grow again. If the monk or nun completely uproots it, he or she will realize nirvana.

33 If a person doesn't want to cut down the tree of sensual love, its branches and leaves will grow to a greater or lesser extent. If our mind is still caught in sensual love, we're still the calf always needing its mother's udder.

PRACTICES

MINDFUL BREATHING

Breathing in, I calm my body.
Breathing out, I smile.
Dwelling in the present moment,
I know this is a wonderful moment.

We can breathe consciously anytime throughout the day. Anytime we're aware of our breathing, we can recite these lines.

"Breathing in, I calm my body." This line is like drinking a glass of cold water. You feel the cool freshness permeating your body. When I breathe in and recite this line, I actually feel the breathing calming my body and mind. "Breathing out, I smile." A smile can relax hundreds of muscles in your face and make you master of yourself. That is why the Buddhas and bodhisattvas are always smiling.

"Dwelling in the present moment, I know this is a wonderful moment." While I sit here, I don't think of anything else. I sit here, and I know where I am. It is a joy to sit, stable and at ease, and return to ourselves—our breathing, our half smile, our true nature. We can appreciate these moments. We can ask ourselves, "If I don't have peace and joy right now, when will I have peace and joy—tomorrow or after tomorrow? What is preventing me from being happy right now?" We can shorten the verses and say, "Calming, smiling; present moment, wonderful moment." Wherever we are, whatever we're doing, we can come back to ourselves and practice conscious breathing.

THE FIVE MINDFULNESS TRAININGS

The Five Mindfulness Trainings are for everyone, monastics and laypeople. Mindfulness is the kind of energy that can help you to go home to yourself, to be in the here and the now, so that you know what to do and what not to do in order to preserve yourself, to build your true home, to transform your afflictions, and to be a home for other people. The Five Mindfulness Trainings are a very concrete way of practicing mindfulness.

Studying the Five Mindfulness Trainings, we see the path of maintaining them as the path of true love. The first training is the practice of love, as are the second, third, fourth, and fifth. Practicing the Mindfulness Trainings makes you holy. Holiness is possible for all of us.

Reverence for Life

THE FIRST MINDFULNESS TRAINING

Aware of the suffering caused by the destruction of life, I am committed to cultivating the insight of interbeing and compassion and learning ways to protect the lives of people, animals, plants, and minerals. I am determined not to kill, not to let others kill, and not to support any act of killing in the world, in my thinking, or in my way of life. Seeing that harmful actions arise from anger, fear, greed, and intolerance, which in turn come from dualistic and discriminative thinking, I will cultivate openness, nondiscrimination, and nonattachment to views in order to transform violence, fanaticism, and dogmatism in myself and in the world.

True Happiness
THE SECOND MINDFULNESS TRAINING

Aware of the suffering caused by exploitation, social injustice, stealing, and oppression, I am committed to practicing generosity in my thinking, speaking, and acting. I am determined not to steal and not to possess anything that should belong to others; and I will share my time, energy, and material resources with those who are in need. I will practice looking deeply to see that the happiness and suffering of others are not separate from my own happiness and suffering; that true happiness is not possible without understanding and compassion; and that running after wealth, fame, power, and sensual pleasures can bring much suffering and despair. I am aware that happiness depends on my mental attitude and not on external conditions, and that I can live happily in the present moment simply by remembering that I already have more than enough conditions to be happy. I am committed to practicing Right Livelihood so that I can help reduce the suffering of living beings on Earth and reverse the process of global warming.

True Love
THE THIRD MINDFULNESS TRAINING

Aware of the suffering caused by sexual misconduct, I am committed to cultivating responsibility and learning ways to protect the safety and integrity of individuals, couples, families, and society. Knowing that sexual desire is not love, and that sexual activity motivated by craving always harms myself as well as others, I am determined not to engage in sexual relations without true love and a deep, long-term commitment made known to my family and friends. I will do everything in my power to protect children from sexual abuse and to prevent couples and families from being broken by sexual misconduct. Seeing that body and mind are one, I am committed to learning appropriate ways to take care of my sexual energy and cultivating loving kindness, compassion, joy, and inclusiveness—which are the four basic elements of true love—for my greater happiness and the greater happiness of others. Practicing true love, we know that we will continue beautifully into the future.

Loving Speech and Deep Listening
THE FOURTH MINDFULNESS TRAINING

Aware of the suffering caused by unmindful speech and the inability to listen to others, I am committed to cultivating loving speech and compassionate listening in order to relieve suffering and to promote reconciliation and peace in myself and among other people, ethnic and religious groups, and nations. Knowing that words can create happiness or suffering, I am committed to speaking truthfully, using words that inspire confidence, joy, and hope. When anger is manifesting in me, I am determined not to speak. I will practice mindful breathing and walking in order to recognize and to look deeply into my anger. I know that the roots of anger can be found in my wrong perceptions and lack of understanding of the suffering in myself and in the other person. I will speak and listen in a way that can help myself and the other person to transform suffering and see the way out of difficult situations. I am determined not to spread news that I do not know to be certain and not to utter words that can cause division or discord. I will practice Right Diligence to nourish my capacity for understanding, love, joy, and inclusiveness, and gradually transform the anger, violence, and fear that lie deep in my consciousness.

Nourishment and Healing
THE FIFTH MINDFULNESS TRAINING

Aware of the suffering caused by unmindful consumption, I am committed to cultivating good health, both physical and mental, for myself, my family, and my society by practicing mindful eating, drinking, and consuming. I will practice looking deeply into how I consume the Four Kinds of Nutriments, namely edible foods, sense impressions, volition, and consciousness. I am determined not to gamble, or to use alcohol, drugs, or any other products that contain toxins, such as certain websites, electronic games, TV programs, films, magazines, books, and conversations. I will practice coming back to the present moment to be in touch with the refreshing, healing, and nourishing elements in me and around me, not letting regrets and sorrow drag me back into the past nor letting anxieties, fear, or craving pull me out of the present moment. I am determined not to try to cover up loneliness, anxiety, or other suffering by losing myself in consumption. I will contemplate interbeing and consume in a way that preserves peace, joy, and well-being in my body and consciousness, and in the collective body and consciousness of my family, my society, and the Earth.

SELECTIVE WATERING

The practice of selective watering allows the positive seeds in us to grow, and gives strength and vitality to the mind. We let the negative seeds rest and allow space for nourishment to enter. Then, when we need to look into a difficult situation, we'll be able to do so with more ease, clarity, and skill.

The person you love has all kinds of seeds in her: joy, suffering, and anger. If you water her anger, then in just five minutes you can bring the anger out in her. If you know how to water the seeds of her compassion, joy, and understanding, then these seeds will blossom. If you recognize the good seeds in her, you are watering her self-confidence and she will become the source of her own happiness as well as yours.

The practice of selective watering has four parts. First, we allow the negative seeds to sleep in our store consciousness and don't give them a chance to manifest; if they manifest too often, their base will be strengthened. Secondly, if a negative seed manifests, we help it go back to sleep as quickly as possible. We can replace it with another mental formation—this is the third practice of right diligence. The fourth practice is that when a good mental formation has manifested, we try to keep it there as long as we can.

It's just like when a good friend comes to visit, the whole house is joyful so we try to persuade him to stay a few more days.

We can help the other person to do the same, to change her mental formations. If anger or fear manifests in her, we can practice watering a good seed in her that will manifest and replace the other mental formation. With the practice and with the help of the Sangha we can help these seeds to have more of a chance to manifest. We can organize our lives in such a way that the good seeds can be touched and watered several times a day. The good seeds that haven't had a chance to manifest, we now give them a chance.

So as to not water the negative seeds in ourselves and each other, we can promise each other, "Darling, I know there is a seed of anger in you. I know that every time I water that seed, you suffer and you make me suffer too. So I make a vow to refrain from watering the seed of anger in you. I also promise not to water the seed of anger in me. Can you make the same commitment? In our daily lives, let's not read, view, or consume anything that waters the seeds of anger and violence in us. You know that the seed of anger in me is quite big enough. Every time you do or say something that waters it, I suffer and I make you suffer. So let's not water these seeds in each other."

METTA MEDITATION

To love is, first of all, to accept ourselves as we actually are. That is why in this meditation on love, "Knowing Thyself" is the first practice of love. When we practice metta, we see the conditions that have caused us to be the way we are. This makes it easy for us to accept ourselves, including our suffering and our happiness.

We begin with an aspiration: "May I be…." Then we transcend the level of aspiration and look deeply at all the positive and negative characteristics of the object of our meditation, in this case, ourselves. The willingness to love is not yet love. We look deeply, with all our being, in order to understand. We don't want to imitate others or strive after some ideal. The practice of love meditation is not auto-suggestion. We don't just repeat the words, "I love myself. I love all beings." We look deeply at our bodies, our feelings, our perceptions, our mental formations, and our consciousness, and in just a few weeks of daily practice our aspiration to love will become a deep intention. Love will enter our thoughts, our words, and our actions, and we will notice that we have become more peaceful, happy, and lighter in body and spirit; safer from injury; and freer from anger, afflictions, fear, and anxiety.

When we practice, we observe how much peace, happiness, and lightness we already have. We notice whether we are anxious about accidents or misfortunes, and how much anger, irritation, fear, anxiety, or worry are already in us. As we become aware of the feelings in us, our self-understanding will deepen. We will see how our fears and lack of peace contribute to our unhappiness, and we will see the value of loving ourselves and cultivating a heart of compassion.

In this meditation on love, "anger, afflictions, fear, and anxiety" refer to all the unwholesome, negative states of mind that dwell in us and rob us of our peace and happiness. Anger, fear, anxiety, craving, greed, and ignorance are the great afflictions of our time. By practicing mindful living, we are able to deal with them, and our love is translated into effective action.

To practice this love meditation, sit still, calm your body and your breathing, and recite it to yourself. The sitting position is a wonderful position for practicing this. Sitting still, you're not too preoccupied with other matters, so you can look deeply at yourself as you are, cultivate your love for yourself, and determine the best ways to express this love in the world.

May I be peaceful, happy, and light in body and spirit.
May she be peaceful, happy, and light in body and spirit.
May he be peaceful, happy, and light in body and spirit.
May they be peaceful, happy, and light in body and spirit.

May I be safe and free from injury.
May she be safe and free from injury.
May he be safe and free from injury.
May they be safe and free from injury.

May I be free from anger, afflictions, fear, and anxiety.
May she be free from anger, afflictions, fear, and anxiety.
May he be free from anger, afflictions, fear, and anxiety.
May they be free from anger, afflictions, fear, and anxiety.

Begin practicing this love meditation on yourself, using the word "I." Until you are able to love and take care of yourself, you cannot be of much help to others. After that, practice on others ("he/she," "they")—first on someone you like, then on someone neutral to you, then on someone you love, and finally on someone the mere thought of whom makes you suffer.

THE FIVE AWARENESSES

These verses can be used by anyone at anytime as a practice to help safeguard our relationships. Many people have used them in weddings and commitment ceremonies and some couples like to recite them together weekly. If you have a bell, you can invite it to sound after you recite each verse. Breathe in and out a few times in silence before going on to the next one.

1 We are aware that all generations of our ancestors and all future generations are present in us.

2 We are aware of the expectations that our ancestors, our children, and their children have of us.

3 We are aware that our joy, peace, freedom, and harmony are the joy, peace, freedom, and harmony of our ancestors, our children, and their children.

4 We are aware that understanding is the very foundation of love.

5 We are aware that blaming and arguing can never help us and only create a wider gap between us; that only understanding, trust, and love can help us change and grow.

BEGINNING ANEW

At Plum Village, we practice a ceremony of Beginning Anew every week. Everyone sits in a circle with a vase of fresh flowers in the center, and we follow our breathing as we wait for the facilitator to begin. The ceremony has three parts: flower watering, expressing regrets, and expressing hurts and difficulties. This practice can prevent feelings of hurt from building up over the weeks and helps make the situation safe for everyone in the community.

We begin with flower watering. When someone is ready to speak, she joins her palms and the others join their palms to show that she has the right to speak. Then she stands, walks slowly to the flowers, takes the vase in her hands, and returns to her seat. When she speaks, her words reflect the freshness and beauty of the flowers that are in her hands. During flower watering, the speaker acknowledges the wholesome, wonderful qualities of the others. It is not flattery; we always speak the truth. Everyone has some strong points that can be seen with awareness. No one can interrupt the person who has the flowers. She is allowed as much time as she needs, and everyone else practices deep listening. When she is finished speaking, she stands up and mindfully returns the vase to the center of the room.

In the second part of the ceremony, we express regret for anything we have done to hurt others. It does not take more than one thoughtless phrase to hurt someone. The ceremony of Beginning Anew is an opportunity for us to recall some regret from earlier in the week and undo it.

In the third part of the ceremony, we express ways in which others have hurt us. Loving speech is crucial. We want to heal the community, not harm it. We speak frankly, but we do not want to be destructive. Listening meditation is an important part of the practice. When we sit in a circle of friends who are all practicing deep listening, our speech becomes more beautiful and more constructive. We never blame or argue.

Compassionate listening is crucial. We listen with the willingness to relieve the suffering of the other person, not to judge or argue with her. We listen with all our attention. Even if we hear something that is not true, we continue to listen deeply so the that other person can fully express her pain and release the tensions within herself. If we reply to her or correct her, the practice will not bear fruit. We just listen. If we need to tell the other person that her perception was not correct, we can do that a few days later, privately and calmly. Then, at the next Beginning Anew session, she may be the person who rectifies the error and we will not have to say anything. We close the ceremony with a song or by sitting together in the circle and breathing for a minute.

HUGGING MEDITATION

Hugging meditation is a practice I invented. In 1966, a woman poet took me to the Atlanta Airport and then asked, "Is it all right to hug a Buddhist monk?" In my country, we are not used to expressing ourselves that way, but I thought, "I am a Zen teacher. It should be no problem for me to do that." So I said, "Why not?" and she hugged me. But I was quite stiff. While on the plane, I decided that if I wanted to work with friends in the West, I would have to learn the culture of the West, so I invented hugging meditation.

Hugging meditation is a combination of East and West. According to the practice, you have to really hug the person you are hugging. You have to make him or her very real in your arms, not just for the sake of appearances, patting him on the back to pretend you are there, but breathing consciously and hugging with all your body, spirit, and heart. Hugging meditation is a practice of mindfulness. "Breathing in, I know my dear one is in my arms, alive. Breathing out, she is so precious to me." If you breathe deeply like that, holding the person you love, the energy of care, love, and mindfulness will penetrate into that person and she will be nourished and bloom like a flower.

PEACE TREATY AND PEACE NOTE

The Peace Treaty is not just a piece of paper; it is a practice that can help us live long and happily together. The treaty has two parts—one for the person who is angry and one for the person who has caused the anger.

Peace Treaty

In Order That We May Live Long and Happily Together, In Order That We May Continually Develop and Deepen Our Love and Understanding, We the Undersigned, Vow to Observe and Practice the Following:

I, the one who is angry, agree to:

1. Refrain from saying or doing anything that might cause further damage or escalate the anger.
2. Not suppress my anger.
3. Practice breathing and taking refuge in the island of myself.
4. Calmly, within twenty-four hours, tell the one who has made me angry about my anger and suffering, either verbally or by delivering a Peace Note.
5. Ask for an appointment for later in the week (e.g.,

Friday evening) to discuss this matter more thoroughly, either verbally or by Peace Note.

6. Not say: "I am not angry. It's okay. I am not suffering. There is nothing to be angry about, at least not enough to make me angry."

7. Practice breathing and looking deeply into my daily life—while sitting, lying down, standing, and walking—in order to see:

   a. the ways I myself have been unskillful at times;

   b. how I have hurt the other person because of my own habit energy;

   c. how the strong seed of anger in me is the primary cause of my anger;

   d. how the other person's suffering, which waters the seed of my anger, is the secondary cause;

   e. how the other person is only seeking relief from his or her own suffering;

   f. that as long as the other person suffers, I cannot be truly happy.

8. Apologize immediately, without waiting until the Friday evening, as soon as I realize my unskillfulness and lack of mindfulness.

9. Postpone the Friday meeting if I do not feel calm enough to meet with the other person.

I, the one who has made the other angry, agree to:

1. Respect the other person's feelings, not ridicule him or her, and allow enough time for him or her to calm down;
2. Not press for an immediate discussion;
3. Confirm the other person's request for a meeting, either verbally or by note, and assure him or her that I will be there;
4. Practice breathing and taking refuge in the island of myself to see how:
   a. I have seeds of unkindness and anger as well as the habit energy to make the other person unhappy;
   b. I have mistakenly thought that making the other person suffer would relieve my own suffering;
   c. by making him or her suffer, I make myself suffer.
5. Apologize as soon as I realize my unskillfulness and lack of mindfulness, without making any attempt to justify myself and without waiting until the Friday meeting.

We Vow, with Lord Buddha as Witness and the Mindful Presence of the Sangha, to Abide by These Articles and to Practice Wholeheartedly. We Invoke the Three Gems for Protection and to Grant Us Clarity and Confidence.

Signed, _____

the Day of _____

in the Year _____

If we, our partners, and our families want not to suffer, not to be caught in blaming and fighting, we can sign this Peace Treaty. According to the fourth article of the treaty, we have up to twenty-four hours to calm ourselves. Then we must tell the other person we are angry. We do not have the right to keep our anger any longer than that. If we do, it becomes poisonous, and it may destroy us and the person we love. If we are used to the practice, we may be ready to tell him in five or ten minutes, but the maximum is twenty-four hours. We can say, "My dear friend, what you said this morning made me very angry. I suffered very much and I want you to know it."

According to the fifth article, we end with this sentence, "I hope that by Friday evening both of us will have had a chance to look deeply into this matter." Then we make an appointment. Friday evening is a good time to defuse all the bombs, big or small, so that we will have the whole weekend for our enjoyment.

If we feel it is not yet safe for us to speak to our partner, if we do not feel capable of doing it in a calm way and the deadline of twenty-four hours is approaching, we can use this "Peace Note":

Peace Note

Date _____

Time _____

Dear _____,This morning (afternoon), you said (did) something that made me very angry. I suffered very much. I want you to know this. You said (did):
Please let us both look at what you said (did) and examine the matter together in a calm and open manner this Friday evening.
Yours, not very happy right now,

_____

A NOTE ON THE TRANSLATION

The Sutra on the Net of Sensual Love was translated from Chinese into Vietnamese from the Dharmapada of the Chinese Canon by Thich Nhat Hanh. Sister Chân Đinh Nghiêm, Sister Chân Hiên Nghiêm, Sister Annabel Laity, and Brother Chân Pháp Luu translated the Sutra into English. Many thanks to Brother Chân Pháp Luu, Sister Annabel Laity, Sister Chân Dinh Nghiem, and Sister Chân Khong for translating the talks used in this book.

The Sutra on the Net of Sensual Love used here is extracted from the Chinese Dharmapada. The Chinese Dharmapada is sutra number 210 in the Taisho Tripitaka. It has 39 chapters with 752 verses. It can be compared with the Chapter on Sensual Love in the Chinese Udanavarga (sutra number 213 in the Revised Tripitaka) and with the Dhammapada of the Pali Canon, which has 26 chapters and 403 verses. The Chinese Dharmapada was translated in the third century c.e., the Udanavarga was translated in the tenth century c.e., so the former sutra preceded it by around seven hundred years.

Parallax Press, a nonprofit organization, publishes books on engaged Buddhism and the practice of mindfulness by Thich Nhat Hanh and other authors. All of Thich Nhat Hanh's work is available at our online store and in our free catalog. For a copy of the catalog, please contact:

Parallax Press
P.O. Box 7355
Berkeley, CA 94707
Tel: (510) 525-0101

www.parallax.org

Monastics and laypeople practice the art of mindful living in the tradition of Thich Nhat Hanh at retreat communities in France and the United States. To reach any of these communities, or for information about individuals and families joining for a practice period, please contact:

Plum Village
13 Martineau
33580 Dieulivol, France
www.plumvillage.org

Blue Cliff Monastery
3 Mindfulness Road
Pine Bush, NY 12566
www.bluecliffmonastery.org
www.deerparkmonastery.org

Deer Park Monastery
2499 Melru Lane
Escondido, CA 92026
www.bluecliffmonastery.org
www.deerparkmonastery.org

The Mindfulness Bell, a Journal of the Art of Mindful Living in the Tradition of Thich Nhat Hanh, is published three times a year by Plum Village. To subscribe or to see the worldwide directory of Sanghas, visit www.mindfulnessbell.org.

RELATED TITLES
FROM PARALLAX PRESS